# RETURN TO EDEN

# Return to Eden

## *new earth community*

PAULA RULE

goldenraytwinflameearthangel.com

Copyright © 2023 by Paula Rule
goldenraytwinflameearthangel.com


All rights reserved. No part of this book may be reproduced in any manner whatsoever without written permission except in the case of brief quotations embodied in critical articles and reviews.

First Printing, 2023

# Contents

*Dedication* vii

Humanity Reset 1

Divine Nature ~ Christ Consciousness 23

Soul Tribes ~ Return to Eden 59

*Journaling* 73
*Meditation and Dream Journal* 75
*Angel Numbers, Signs and Symbols* 81
*My Path to New Earth Community* 87
*Afterword* 95
*About The Author* 96
*Other Books By Paula Rule* 99

# Dedication

For my Nanna and Poppa.

I was a young girl when I stayed with my grandparents for a night. Their humble home was immaculately clean and quiet. There was no need for words as the silence was golden. The vibration of love they shared included me.

They transcended this realm years ago but appeared to me in a significant dream at the very beginning of my Twin Flame journey.

Spiritual beauty in hearts of Gold.

# Humanity Reset

At the dawn of time the snake made known that we had a choice. We could remain in the perfect coherence of God's garden or we could choose to go down to lower energies. As soon as our progenitors chose to step down from being One with God they became slaves to sin.

They began hurting each other and destroying our world. No longer guided by spirit, they became enamoured with their bodies and opened their minds to evil of every kind. Humans became so beaten down that they traded their God given gifts for money. They cheapened and debased themselves for pieces of paper made by man to enslave the masses. Since then we have been imprisoned in an ego matrix by low vibrational beings who blinded us to our glory, robbed us of our joy and forced us to harm ourselves and each other.

> *For the love of money is a root of all kinds of evil. Some people, eager for money, have wandered from the faith and pierced themselves with many grief's.*
>
> *1 Timothy 6:10*

As we awaken our awareness is opening to the universal chakras. Physical chakras encourage focus on the body and its base is claimed to be the root chakra. Focus on the genital area encourages some to obsess with sex. Therefore people have degraded intercourse to the equivalent of a seven mile run, stress relief and fuck buddies. Sex is also used for power, control and manipulation. Social disease is rampant and unwanted babies are murdered in the millions. We lowered ourselves down to a sad shadow of our long forgotten radiance.

The ego matrix is a manipulation of the mind. From birth we are numbered and named. We grow in toxic soil, bullied into 'fitting in' to the slave mass delusion, that we have to step on our fellow man and applaud fake, selfish hedonists broadcast to the masses. Our minds are deadened through pharmaceuticals and programmed through television, internet and video games; crushing the human spirit through various systems from birth to death.

The enemy turned our paradise into a living hell of injustice and suffering that we had to endure or ignore. Those 'in power' over us are demon possessed entities inhabiting a body, so discernment is required. Any 'people' who harm the innocent are not children of God. Be wary of interacting with these entities as the devil has many tricks to lower your vibration, keep you trapped in unhealthy situations and steal your divine birthright. This is done at the micro and macro level; one on one destruction or mass psyops.

The UFO phenomenon is one such trick. I was into all that stuff years ago until I had a close encounter myself. I was excited to see the craft and open to receiving whatever message came from the stars. They telepathically told me I could go with them in that moment, all I had to do was agree. It would have been an easy way out because enemies were all around me. Instantly, I thought of the bible verse; You will be hated by everyone because of me, but one who stands firm to the end will be saved. I said no, and the UFO disappeared from the sky.

For those poor humans fully involved in the matrix, governments are now offering 'assisted suicide'; murder, in actuality. Just because the enemy is making life unbearable in their matrix is no excuse to hurt yourself. Suicide is not an option – Remember:

This consciousness is a sacred journey that leads to universal truth. We are given a physical body to feel and experience what we need to awaken and ascend. Many situations involve other souls who are predestined to learn and share through interaction with us. Some karmic lessons leave us feeling alone and unable to go on. How can anyone understand what we have endured?

Your brothers and sisters understand better than you may think. You are not alone in your suffering; it is only your thoughts that require elevating. Telling yourself that you somehow deserve to die is evil and pollutes what you share. When you understand that you are in control of your thoughts, you can choose Christ Consciousness.

Christ Consciousness chooses forgiveness over revenge, shows respect rather than hatred, elects dignity through grief and reaches out from heart purity to heal the brokenness in others. When you know your worth it's natural to rise above negativity and be strong enough to be there for those on your soul path.

In the beast system you are expected to interact with *artificial* intelligence in a *virtual* reality. In this false construct you are punished for telling the truth. You grieve the loss of humankind that the beast kills by the millions. Righteous anger at blatant injustice. Frustration and sorrow dealing with closed hearts and deceived minds.

> *If you should suffer for righteousness' sake, you are blessed. And do not be afraid of their threats, nor be troubled.* 1 Peter 3:14

Wallowing in guilt, self-pity or any detrimental emotion keeps you imprisoned in negativity and just lowers and wastes precious energy. Your conscience is your guide, and feeling guilt is a good sign that you are aware of your mistake. Yes, we all have sinned, but those who are spiritually aware understand that acknowledging mistakes and making amends is the golden path to healing and forgiveness.

What is sin? It is not living your divinity or honouring the holiness in your brothers and sisters. Sin is hurting yourself or others. and the one you hurt the most is always yourself. The control matrix has twisted and used the idea of sin to brainwash us into believing we're weak and not good enough. Many give up and begin to love their sins as they feel doomed anyway. Human beings choosing to stay in low vibration choose suffering on the karmic wheel. For those of us ready to transcend the matrix, there is so much more to know and remember about our divine origin and destiny.

Was our collective memory wiped in the past? Some researchers have put forth this theory and could it be true? Ancient peoples have handed down stories of prior resets dating back to the mists of time. How many resets have there been? Have we had chances during past resets to ascend lower energies? It seems every time we have lacked the ability to discern what was best for us. Is this from generational reliance on the matrix mind?

Ancient structures and artefacts reveal advanced civilizations; but they all fell, many leaving no clues as to why. The 'rise and fall' of civilizations show us that these are temporary constructs of hierarchy, where a few destroy the lives of many until that system collapses and a new 'civilization' takes its place. Nothing is civilized in these ego matrixes, but they seem to be all the majority can remember.

Look at the Mayan 'civilization' for example. The people were expected to sacrifice themselves or their children to 'appease' the gods. Archaeologists say their civilization fell because of famine or natural disaster. Maybe the people got sick of living in fear and witnessing their loved ones murdered by a tyrannical few.

Did the tribes we are aware of, merely re-inhabit even more ancient ruins? Some ancient engineering still functions to this day, such as water distribution techniques, made to work in concert with nature, that our society can't seem to replicate. At some points in our mysterious past we created in harmony with divine design. Did those ancestors ascend?

The only peoples left from the past are those who chose to be 'primitive', living in correspondence with nature. Dark forces have done all they can to kill these people, destroy their heritage and force them to depend on a system that takes away their human rights. Only a few of these pure souls are left to guide humanity towards freedom.

In times of change we look to the Bible for guidance and most of it resonates with the heart chakra and strengthens our spirits, but have important scriptures been altered? The unscrupulous have tampered with the Bible for ages. Especially scripture about our origins. For example, does woman come from a mans rib; or is man birthed from a woman's yoni? Women are carers and nurturers, so is it likely Eve would confront a snake, or does it make more sense for Adam to converse with, and be tricked by the snake?

As we have seen, men have been at the apex of the matrix and the 'women' they put forth as examples for us are soulless, surgically altered men. The book of Genesis says man has 'dominion over animals' and so men torture and kill animals for fun or food. We instinctively know this is wrong; we were given stewardship of earth and her creatures.

The whole mainstream setup is a lie and only those who benefit from the lie want us trapped in it; but their latest 'reset' coincides with our great awakening ~ to the truth. Of who we are, who we were and who we are made to be in the power of the Holy Spirit. Love is who we are. And what we create with love is beautiful.

We are gifted and talented in unique ways that benefit each other, our planet and our universe. We have been born throughout the ages to share sacred love and happiness. The most powerful force on the planet comes from the heart and when that energy is shared, it's multiplied. Be yourself and share your unique expression of divine love.

Universal light is enabling and accelerating our spiritual growth at this time. Through these upgrades, deep emotions related to ancient pain are released through memories and tears. Forgive yourself and let go. Those situations only hurt so much because you cared. Surrender all hurt and regret from the past. It's time to be kind and gentle with yourself and really feel the love that is your key to rising above the ego matrix. Universal light shines on your golden heart and the darkness falls like seeds to the earth. Your sacred offering yields a harvest of divine beauty that is yours forever - and you are free.

Strip away all that weighs you down and enter naked into the pure waters of soul baptism. Emerge a divine golden angel vibrating to the frequency of universal love. Everything you were, are, and becoming is all coming together in the eternal Now. Universal love and light reset the frequency and vibration of our human form.

As you let go and let love lead, you can see your old boundaries clearly and choose to release negative patterns your ego made to protect itself. The true self is a wondrous discovery of complete beauty created for ecstatic union.

Integrate the lessons you came here to learn and grow more aware and powerful than before; grateful for every experience your soul needs to flower in your unique expression of Christ Consciousness.

The pure love vibrating from your heart makes angels, saints and ancestors cheer you on, sharing their transcendental love with you. When your life is your prayer you achieve your dreams; create miracles, open hearts and touch souls intimately with your prayers, thoughts, words and deeds.

> *You are like the wings of a dove covered with silver, and its pinions with glistening gold.* Psalm 68:13

---

The mind is a direct link to universal wisdom. This is why individuals considered geniuses, all credit dreams or visions for their work. Einstein, Edward Case, Nicola Tesla and Srinivasa Ramanujan for example. These people understood they were merely a conduit for higher intelligence. If they had been stressing about the past or worried about the future they would not have been open channels for divine downloads.

> *Therefore I tell you, do not worry about your life, what you will eat or drink, what you will wear. Is not life more than food and the body more than clothes? Consider how the lilies of the field grow; they do not labour or spin. Yet I tell you that not even Solomon in all his glory was adorned like one of these.* Matthew 6:25-29

You are supposed to live in the moment, not the matrix mind. In the moment is where your senses are engaged, intuition is heightened and inspiration is natural. The mind is alert and open to connection with universal energy and for prayer, with the urging of the heart. Your heartfelt prayer makes you a star. The Lord Himself is your audience and delights in your offering.

We are literally born again in the Age of Aquarius. The suffering of the past is over as mankind grows strong in spirit and whole in divine nature...as we were always meant to be. This is the mass awakening and Twin Flames light the way.

> *Twin Flames are the lock and the key that together open the way to humanity's transformation and transcendence beyond the ego. The moment of conscious joining (on any level of consciousness) turns the key in the lock. The moment you connect, whether together physically or in higher consciousness, you are eligible for direct delivery of pure light.* Twin Flame Physics, Angelina Heart.

Twin Flame awakening is through instant recognition of your soul in another. This activates ancient DNA for the recollection of our true power and the purpose of divine love. This journey begins with healing of self.

Spiritual love that transcends time and space is the new currency of intimate communities worldwide. This is why the Twin Flame dynamic is so important for our ascension. The Twin Flame mission is foremost. To unite with a Twin is the icing on the cake...possible but not certain in these end times. One Twin has lived from the spirit and the other from the ego. The spiritual Twin awakens the ego Twin to their own divinity and that of humanity.

Both Twins are called to release the past and create life anew in Christ Consciousness. The ego matrix Twin may not choose this genesis - and that is their choice. The spiritual Twin continues the mission for both as this is a huge step up on the soul path. It's not just an intimate relationship with God anymore, it's reaching out to brothers and sisters in spirit for the creation of new earth community.

My Twin is a slave to the beast system. Living a lie from fear. He is a mainstream doctor yet he joined with other powerful men to try to destroy me in body and name. I've never seen anyone gaze at me with such longing as my Twin, but he would rather hide away in his ivory tower and take no responsibility for his actions, than tell the truth.

It would be crazy for me to have anything to do with someone who proved to be corrupt and willing and able to harm innocents to cover abuse. I can't even think of my Twin as a man. He is a brick in the wall, cog in the wheel and traitor to humanity.

That's why it can take a miracle for Twin Union in the beast system and why I wrote Divine Love Twin Flames with quotes from A Course in Miracles by Paula Rule. I share the quotes that enabled me to reach out to my Twin and begin my part of our work for humanity.

I had to rise above what my Twin did to me and extend the truth of divine love to him. A Course in Miracles states that 'perfect love is the atonement.' And so it is. To merge with me, my Twin would have to make right what he did to me.

*Let not the form of his mistakes keep you from him whose holiness is yours. Beyond his errors is his holiness and your salvation.* ACIM quote Divine Love Twin Flames by Paula Rule.

Now we are free from illusion and ready for the freedom, bliss and abundance of real living, sharing divine love with our brothers and sisters.

I shared divine love with my late husband, Chris. The moment we met true love blossomed. Our soul mate union healed us both and we knew how blessed we were. People said I saved his soul. No, he already had the most beautiful soul I've ever known. Deep respect grew to complete awe for his mind blowing courage and dignity during the most difficult test of all. It was his example that made me strong and together we fulfilled the Lord's Template for Divine Love.

It is my Twin's soul I have been called to help save. He has the free will to be as he chooses and so far he has chosen the way of the snake; a self serving, deceptive, callous hypocrite that only the spirit of Christ can save. The Divine Masculine is open, honest, loving and caring. He stands for truth and would give his life to save the souls of others. Divine Masculine is when you can see Jesus in him.

Those choosing to live in Christ Consciousness show the way for us to leave the ego matrix behind, creating new earth communities of love and abundance for all.

*Come out of her, my people so that you will not share in her sins, so that you will not receive any of her plagues.* Revelation 18:4

Human beings still have a choice; a last choice, to stay in the beast system or leave their corrupt cities and live in our own communities, grow our own food, caring for our planet, ourselves and each other. Gaia calls us home to her heart; to her mountains and beaches, forests, flowers, rivers and streams; - back to nature where we belong.

The remnants of humanity carry our greatest treasure within ourselves. We did not take the beast's mark and operating system. Our ascension is assured as we reconnect with our inborn operating system. We are blessed with the Holy Spirit and the innate desire to shine with pure love.

We never again trust in man to tell us what to do. We connect to divine guidance. We ask the Lord for justice and it is delivered. Dark forces will not be able to harm our souls in the shared energy of Christ Consciousness.

*He will judge between the nations and will settle disputes for many peoples. They will beat their swords into plowshares and their spears into pruning hooks. Nation will not take up sword against nation, nor will they train for war anymore.* Isaiah 2:4

The beast matrix is self destructing as the children of God move away to begin anew in the Aquarian age of enlightenment. We recall our divine nature and purpose; and that is love.

Despite the control system destroying humanity since the beginning of creation, Christ Consciousness is our genesis and our destiny. Jesus demonstrated with His life that we are made for divine love and miracles. Through the Holy Spirit we know the truth. We are spiritual light beings. What joy when we all glow with the light of Christ Consciousness! The great awakening calls humanity to reset to our natural operating system ~ the life of the spirit, connection from the heart and joy of the moment that lasts forever.

*And now, dear brothers and sisters, one final thing. Fix your thoughts on what is true, and honorable, and right, and pure, and lovely, and admirable. Think about things that are excellent and worthy of praise.* Philippians 4:8

# Divine Nature ~ Christ Consciousness

We were made to be divine in nature, living in harmony with Gaia and her creatures. The world was completely abundant and we were high on love and happiness. Created to live in purity and spiritual ecstasy, born with all we need to grow in spirit for our brief time in a human body. When we connect through the crown chakra to universal wisdom and share from the heart chakra, we base our society on love and transform our planet into the paradise it was always meant to be.

The color of our skin, geographic location or how we worship were mere perceptions within the old ego based matrix. Our minds and hearts are opening to the truth and beauty of the light beings we really are. For those of us ready to transcend the matrix, there is so much more to know and remember about our celestial origin and destiny.

We activate each other for the revelation of powerful abilities that lay dormant in the ego matrix. We understand that miracles occur through love. Christ Consciousness is the foundation for ascension as cosmic energy awakens us to our purpose in the new earth paradigm.

Most people have a mental block when they think of Jesus. They have grown up in a system that made his image into an idol, misrepresented his example to cause division and murdered innocents in his name.

Jesus followed his soul path to heal the sick, work miracles and open the hearts of billions for the salvation of humanity. The Holy Spirit activates his divine connection with us. We are guided and protected as he was…our hearts beating with happiness and thanks for his life.

He was born into the injustice and suffering of the ego matrix with awareness of his soul purpose. His heavenly Father instructed him to teach us the truth of our power but only those who were pure of heart could begin to understand and try to follow him.

He grew through experience. He felt hunger, cold, exhaustion and pain through devotion to his path. Caring for his brothers and sisters in spirit amplified his knowledge of love, sorrow, joy and grief. He taught spiritual truth and worked miracles of healing, advocating for those suffering injustice. A call to Christ Consciousness is a call to action; to demonstrate universal Love.

He did not cater to the ego trips of others and spoke out against the hypocrisy of ruling religious leaders, saying, "You snakes! You brood of vipers! How will you escape being condemned to hell? Matthew 23:33.

He lost patience with the disciples who were still slaves to cultural conditioning, doubt and fear, exclaiming, "O faithless generation, how long shall I be with you? How long shall I suffer you?" Mark 9:19.

His disciples stabbed him in the back and ran away when He was in trouble. Matthew 26:16, Mark 14:50. Most people only followed him because he gave them bread and then screamed for his death when He didn't. John 6:26, Luke 23:21-23. During the worst night of his life he asked his friends to stay awake with him and they couldn't even do that. Matthew 26:40.

He knew he would soon be murdered and left them with instruction for awakening and ascension. "A new command I give you: love one another. As I have loved you, so you must love one another." John 13:34. Just before he was killed he turned to some women and said, "Daughters of Jerusalem, do not weep for me; weep for yourselves and for your children.' Luke 23:28.

He was hit with hatred and rejection from the powerful in the ego matrix...as are we who follow Him. We are a mirror to those who don't want to see how negative their presence is. They may break the mirror but they can't erase the reflection of beauty, glory and fulfilment they glimpsed in themselves.

He came to show us the way to be truly human; to attune with the spiritual and transcend the ego matrix. To be and become all we were created for. The prayer he taught us demonstrates our divine origin. Our Father who is in Heaven, Holy is your name. Your kingdom come, Your will be done, on earth as it is in heaven....Matthew 6:9-10

Thank you Jesus for showing us we are eternal, spiritual light beings; here only for a brief time to help each other rise above the matrix to our home of universal love. We are continually evolving in the spirit of Christ so basic awareness of traits and abilities innate in humans is helpful. Let's start with

*The Clairs*

Clair as a prefix means clear. So the 'Clairs' are part of our operating system when we become clear channels for healing, transmutation, divination, revelation and more...

Inner vision is known as Clairvoyance - the ability to see through time and space through the power of the third eye.

Clairsentience understands by feeling the vibrations of others, plants, animals, Gaia and the Cosmos.

Clairaudience is the ability to discern truth and hear clear messages from the spiritual realm.

Clairtangency is downloading information through touching an object or person.

We each have some of these gifts for personal enlightenment and to share for the benefit of all. In Christ Consciousness we are who we are.

*The World of Dreams*

When the mind is at rest, dreams come as a gift; to inspire, see solutions or as a warning of danger. They are integral to the human experience and described within the old and new testament. Daniel, for example, interpreted a king's dreams with God's help, to save the lives of others and was promoted. Joseph was warned by an angel in a dream to leave before the Christ child could be killed. As long as humanity has existed we have dreamed. Here's an example of one of my recurring and progressive dreams -

Years ago I began to dream of being in a deserted mansion with huge open windows. Sheer white lace curtains moved gently with the sighs of the wind. I wandered through empty rooms knowing I somehow belonged there. At significant times in my life I'd find myself in that dreamscape again, feeling the familiarity of home, though I never encountered another soul.

I hadn't visited that space for ages but recently I was there again.This time I was on the roof surrounded by people.There was life and movement - something big was happening. A bad man picked up my baby to throw down to the ground but he fell instead.The crowd was cheering and I awoke with great happiness and confidence.

After all these years my dream had a happy ending. Thank You my Father – King of the Universe.

*Astral Alignment*

The universe and everything in it also affects our identity and evolution. The planets and their positions in the sky have been of great interest since ancient times. A star lead wise men from the east to the birthplace of Jesus where they gave the Christ child precious gifts. He was born into the age of Pisces, known as the age of suffering.

> *When they saw the star, they were overjoyed.* Matthew 2:10

For aeons, constellations present at birth have been noted and associated with specific personality traits attributed to what we call star signs. We can now view these traits from higher perspective to share quality love and affection. All negative traits attributed to star signs must go as this only gets in the way of you shining and completing your soul journey.

They are grouped into fundamental elements of our earth. Water and earth signs are feminine energy and fire and air signs are seen as masculine energy. For a more rounded insight, they are also grouped into modalities of cardinal, fixed and mutable signs. Basically, cardinal energy creates change, fixed signs implement the new and mutable signs are open to all possibilities. The cardinal signs are Aries, Capricorn, Libra and Cancer. The fixed signs are Leo, Taurus, Aquarius and Scorpio. The mutable signs are Sagittarius, Virgo, Gemini and Pisces.

*Earth Signs*

Taurus ~ The flowering of love is my delight.

Virgo ~ My soul is complete in everlasting love.

Capricorn ~ I provide comfort and love; my hearth is your home.

*Water Signs*

Cancer ~ My sacred heart is your home.

Scorpio ~ Intimate knowledge of life, death and ecstasy.

Pisces ~ I am purified and restored in eternal love.

*Air Signs*

Gemini ~ I embody the integration of natural duality.

Libra ~ I share love that legends are made of. Natural justice is my forte.

Aquarius ~ My love is beyond your wildest dreams.

*Fire Signs*

Leo ~ I share fiery passion and protect you with my life.

Sagittarius ~ I set your heart ablaze with passion.

Aries ~ My soul is reborn through passionate intensity.

You may exhibit some or all of these traits...how did the stars grace the sky at your moment of birth and how did their energy influence your journey?

At the time of my birth a Grand Square, Mystic Rectangle and two Stelliums between earth and water were present. Virgo and Pisces energies connected and balanced on many energetic levels. The love of my life was written in the stars when I took physical form and entered the matrix. Meeting, marrying and caring for Chris until he died in my arms was truly the completion of love.

Flowers, gemstones and colours have all been connected with star signs throughout the ages. We are symbiotically connected to the beauty of nature.

*Numbers*

Numerology, mathematical arrangements and golden ratio can be messages to guide us. Angel numbers are manifesting everywhere, they represent specific messages to assist us but are they also to impress the importance of numerical sequences?

> *To understand the universe, think in terms of energy, frequency and vibration. The significance of the 3, 6, and 9.* Nikola Tesla

Some have theorised that the universe is made of mathematics and we see sacred geometry all around us. A book of numbers is included in the Bible so this concept is important in universal energy and can also been seen in signs and symbols. One such symbol is the star tetrahedron.

*Symbols /Sacred Geometry - Star Tetrahedron*

This ancient symbol of sacred geometry has various meanings, many lost to the ages. In our time this image is seen as integration and elevation of masculine and feminine energies. It also illustrates energetic configurations of soul mates and twin flames. The upright pyramid represents true soul mate love, where two physical beings emit a shared high vibration frequency, connecting with the energy of the One. The inverted pyramid is the Twin Flame code activation of universal self. Two eternal souls manifest their unique celestial energetic signature in the physical world to become One - anchoring the vibration of divine love on earth.

Sacred geometry has always been present and is well known now through displays of cymatics, where a crystal or surface is vibrated at various frequencies to assemble particles in patterns.

It has also been demonstrated that water exposed to loving human intention results in exquisite physical molecular formations in the water. Water exposed to human low vibration results in ugly growths. This is a perfect example of why high vibration is so important. We are energetic conductors influencing the environment that surrounds us.

*Rainbow Rays*

The ancient association of the body's seven chakras and the seven colours of the rainbow is a sign in the 3D to upgrade our natural energy to open to the light of universal rainbow rays. A rainbow is somehow sacred to us and regarded as a miracle of hope and symbol of universal love and abundance. As above, so below.

From prehistoric times rainbow colors have been associated with the physical chakras, and transcendental chakras are linked with the properties of precious metals. These energy centres are overseen by an Archangel or Ascended Master you connect with through prayer and the presence of related crystals increases power and focus. Awareness expands to encompass the psychic self where you may be drawn to a specific color indicating your energetic signature. Inner work purifies and enhances the gifts of that frequency.

You may heal and activate more than one ray for your ascension. Over many lifetimes you may project the aura of one or several colors of the rainbow spectrum. At the end of the rainbow is a pot of gold representing the Golden Ray of Christ Consciousness.

Through the foundational modality of meditation; physical, emotional and spiritual healing are attained. You glow with wisdom, shining your individual light with awakened brothers and sisters to co create a rainbow star soul harmonic vibrational bridge to the heart of the galaxy. When we heal and refine the energies of the heart chakra, all the body's energy centres align for optimal health. Then we easily connect to the transcendental chakras for universal wisdom and expansion.

## *Meditation/Breath Work*

Breath work is integral to healing the body, mind and soul. Regulation of breathing enhances awareness in the moment, focuses attention and calms the mind. To train the body for deep breathing, silently repeating a phrase on inhale and/or exhale, such as , 'I love you Jesus', is helpful in the beginning of your meditation practice. Focus is then on healing the body, releasing negativity, expanding consciousness or whatever is your focus in the moment.

Meditation in nature is super healthy. If you meditate indoors, silence or natural rhythms such as new age music can assist in a deep meditative state. Visualisation is helpful to focus on healing specific ailments or manifest optimum outcomes. In the meditative state, visualisations can happen naturally, showing you what you need to know. Guided meditation is also helpful in certain situations.

Lotus position is not necessary. I have dissolved blood clots, managed intense pain, cleared skin conditions, gained insights to complex problems and reset and rejuvenated my system in prone position. Physical, mental and spiritual healing can be attained through breath work and the practice of meditation.

*Without full awareness of breathing, there can be no development of meditative stability and understanding.* Thich Nhat Hanh.

## *Heart Chakra – Universal CPU*

Our heartbeat is designed to synchronize with Gaia and the universe. Ancient peoples knew the heart chakra as the seat of intelligence. Jesus is depicted with a Sacred Heart, displaying the divine significance of the heart chakra. He came to demonstrate this truth so we may remember and engender universal principles.

When we really feel love and positive emotions we are sending an electromagnetic frequency that is received, creating a positive energetic connection. The heart chakra is our sacred way of communication and communion with our brothers and sisters.

When we connect through the heart chakra; different perceptions, locations or languages are no barrier as no words are needed... Our real power resides in our hearts.

## *Earth Star Chakra*

The earth star chakra beneath the feet is your energetic connection to mother earth. Align your physical body by walking barefoot in grass or hugging a tree, swimming in the ocean or indeed any action that honours our planet. Communicate with nature by sending positive vibrations to the plants and creatures who share our Garden of Eden. The love of Gaia is ancient sacred knowledge for ascension so feel the earth's resonance vibrating through your chakras to integrate optimal health and vitality. As we heal our earth we heal ourselves.

## Spirit Chakra

Connection to the realm of spirit highlights your spiritual gifts and abilities. There is no judgement or linear time here so you are free to embrace and refine your skills of clairvoyance, clairaudience, clairsentience and claircognizance. This magical kingdom is also home to your spirit animals and kindred spirits from beyond time and space.

*Soul Star Chakra*

Your illuminated self is accessed through an energetic field in the ether above the crown chakra. Activating this chakra consolidates your experiences in the ego matrix from your ancient, modern and timeless self. Personal identity is strengthened and expanded as you integrate the truth that you are a star soul in a universe of divine love. Spiritually advanced souls are often depicted with a halo of white or golden light above their heads representing the significance of soul star activation.

*Universal Soul Chakra*

Becoming a master of the world within and without through transmutation of lower energy fields. Adherence to universal law yields extraordinary power to co-create an eternal masterpiece of celestial love. This cosmic unified energy often heralds the awakening of the Twin Flame archetype. Transformation from I AM to We Are One.

*Divine Stellar Gateway Chakra*

Christ Consciousness is One with the Creator of All. Mastery of the ego self and perfect alignment with Divine Will is the power to manifest blessing and miracles of love and unity. This Holy Light being has overcome the karmic wheel for the ascension of all.

Trust and peace go hand in hand, so hold the hand of divine guidance. Your journey to the Now moment leads to miracles beyond your wildest dreams. Awakening to your multidimensional identity is a revelation and evolution of soul. Divine child, the dignity of a beautiful spirit is yours forever.

*I relax in the depths of universal wisdom and go with the flow of divine love.* Paula Rule

*Historical Twin Flames*

The Twin Flame dynamic is not new, these souls have been connecting for ages. Historical Twin Flames, living from Christ Consciousness set up new earth communities for centuries but did so in the mainstream and therefore had to follow rules dictated by others in the hierarchy of evil. These advanced souls participated in miracles, experienced higher love and life to the full. Here are a few examples from Jesus and Mary to the present day:

*Jesus and Mary*

The light of his sacred heart was a mirror to her. She could see how she had darkened her soul in the matrix and vowed to dedicate her life to love. She proved her devotion by washing His feet with expensive perfume, demonstrating her choice to leave the mainstream for good.

After His death; the patriarchal state twisted and used the power of Christianity. Mary was sent away and arrogant males began a system based on control and deception. To love God and live from the higher chakras you had to be celibate, segregated from the opposite sex and separated from society. Suffering and deprivation was the order of the day.

*St Paula and St Jerome*

She was a wealthy young widow who travelled to the Holy Land where she was inspired to create Christian retreats with Saint Jerome. He was a priest, hermit, scholar and writer. Paula helped Jerome in his translation of the Bible. They pursued a destitute lifestyle. Sadly, many were jealous of their mystical connection.

When Paula died, Jerome buried her in the holiest place he could think of - beneath the altar of the Church of the Nativity. When Jerome died, his friends buried him close to her.

*St Francis and St Clare*

Though attracted to her beauty, he had no desire to leave his position of wealth and ease. In time his heart was opened by Jesus. He completely changed his life. Now attuned to Universal wisdom, he began his holy mission. His soul growth attracted Clare and elevated her mission to establish a home for spiritual women and the poor.

*St Mary MacKillop and Julian Woods*

Priest, Julian Tenison Woods and Sister Mary MacKillop founded the Sisters of St Joseph in Australia. Mary and Julian's community emphasized poverty, faith and travel. They helped people in the isolated outback, living as they lived.

Mainstream religions used these light beings to further their own agenda. They dismissed Mary and portrayed Jesus as something we could never be. He came as a man to show us that we are created to be pure in spirit.

The enemy called those who loved like Jesus, 'saints' so we would believe that they were somehow above us and we could never achieve their status. Saints are people just like us who are inspired to choose the soul path. In Christ Consciousness they overcome difficulty, heal others and perform miracles. We revere these beloved brothers and sisters for their courage and devotion. The power of the Holy Spirit is revealed through their lives and they become an example for us.

Many Twins are now realising this journey is about universal love for all brothers and sisters in spirit through the founding of new earth. Imagine us all living in paradise, valued for our unique skills and abilities and loved for who we are. I see us all laughing with happiness and thrilled to be together. The Lord is with us on a spiritual high beyond all we have known.

The physical body is seen as a vehicle to complete the tasks assigned for restoration of humanity and ascension, to co create life and feel the joy of giving, caring, loving and sharing. When we live from the higher chakras we understand that lovemaking is sacred and only shared in love. Sacred Sexuality is created by the universe, written in the stars, encoded in your DNA and accessed through the higher chakras to take you out of this world through the portal of ecstasy. There is nothing more beautiful than true love.

## The Alchemy of Celibacy

Sacred Sexuality is the physical expression of divine love. The 'need' for sex is a sign of being locked into the lower chakras. Through awakening and ascension; times of celibacy are a powerful tool for energetic reset and elevation. As we raise our frequency and vibration we function more from the higher chakras.

You set standards for yourself and the foundation is self-respect. Revel in self-care and spoil yourself. Go within to meditate on your soul path with an open and trusting heart, and relax.

These practices lead to self-mastery and empowerment. The beauty of purity shining from you, creates a cleansing and revitalizing energy within a sacred space of safety and truth, that is healing for you and all you love.

*Soul Mates and Twin Flames*

Your soul mate is someone you trust and respect as this person embodies all the qualities you admire. It is like you have known and loved them forever. These people validate your ego self, consolidating experience that facilitates mutual growth. Through the course of your life you may have more than one for soul expansion.

A Twin is your cosmic mirror. The connection is profound and undeniable. It is the highest energy for remembering and becoming your universal self formed in the galaxies beyond time and space. The ego self is overcome and released as universal love electrifies your chakras for ultimate awakening and ascension.

Divine love partnership grows through the power of the Holy Spirit and blossoms into Christ Consciousness. I shared divine love with my late husband, Chris. When we met, it was love at first sight. Deep respect grew to complete awe for his mind blowing courage and dignity during the most difficult test of all. Our soul mate union healed us both and we knew how blessed we were. People said I saved his soul. No, he already had the most beautiful soul I've ever known. Caring for Chris until he died in my arms was an honour. It was his example that made me strong and together we fulfilled the Lord's Template for Divine Love.

It is my Twin's soul I have been called to help save. He has the free will to be as he chooses and so far he has chosen the way of the snake. His path is his responsibility - new earth community is my mission.

Now, we are led by the Holy Spirit to embody and experience the return to the divine nature of our species. We were designed to make love, be born into a loving family and grow in love for our brief time in a physical body. We weren't born in sin, we were born into a system of sin. There is only one way out of the beast system, and that is through Jesus.

*Jesus answered, "I am the way and the truth and the life. No one comes to the Father except through me.* John 14:6

He was born of the spirit and His life is the example of how to ascend the matrix. He showed us that all we need is the eternal wisdom that comes from God, who created us to be organic intelligent beings as an integral part of a great ecosystem. He showed us that our lives matter, our treasure is in our hearts and we are powerful creators and miracle workers. He was destined to suffer in the age of Pisces – for us. Now in the Age of Aquarius our minds are clear. Any needless suffering comes from the enemy – not yourself or your brothers and sisters in spirit.

Christ Consciousness is when Jesus lives in your heart. You understand that only doing what is right and good is all you need to be whole and complete in spirit – as you were made to be. Adhering to your soul path empowers you to help others. It's like you've grown rainbow wings to lift and enhance your unique skills, abilities and confidence to a higher level.

Through the Holy Spirit we have direct connection to universal love and the wisdom of Christ Consciousness; where our errors are learning experiences that guide us to the purity and beauty of spirit that is our birthright and eternal joy.

*But the Helper, the Holy Spirit, whom the Father will send in my name, he will teach you all things and bring to your remembrance all that I have said to you.*

John 14:2

Your open heart is the connection where you are One with the highest frequency of universal power. Your pure and innocent love is how you create the life of your dreams, where every moment is treasured forever. It really is that simple. Ecstatic love is what you are created for. Jesus left you with His Holy Spirit, an eternal connection with universal truth to show the way.

*for it is written: "Be holy, because I am holy."* 1 Peter 1:16

Jesus said we must be like little children to enter the Kingdom of God. Being present in the moment, feeling everything with openness, curiosity and wonder. Trusting divine providence without even thinking about it.

Living in the moment is where life happens. You are open and receptive to the stimuli around you and a direct channel for universal wisdom. Fully engaging the senses in nature is powerful. Rediscover secrets of the ancients as universal wisdom plants dreams in your heart. And what you dream, you can create.

Trusting your intuition shows where you are in alignment or where you have more to learn. Being in constant connection with the heart of the universe is the energy where miracles are natural.

Align with your soul path. Activate transcendental chakras to discover and develop spiritual gifts and abilities. Explore the Rainbow Rays of Universal Self. Embrace Christ Consciousness and manifest miracles. Join with brothers and sisters in spirit to create new earth communities.

Jesus called himself the 'Son of man' to demonstrate the trust of a child. A trust in universal wisdom; to show us the pure and powerful miracle workers we are. Together, we are the body of Christ on earth.

> *Don't you know that you yourselves are God's temple and that God's Spirit dwells in your midst?* 1 Corinthians 3:16

In Christ Consciousness, we restore our world to the balance of divine love. Imagine everyone wanting only to master their soul path and share deep love for eternity. Do you feel the excitement of universal upgrades through the crown chakra? Is your heart chakra open and clear to embrace the warmth of divine love - and share that light? Are you prepared for the Golden Age of Christ Consciousness? Only when we join together in harmony will the seeds of new earth grow to fruition.

Precious child of God, you are here to embody the bliss of ascension. When you know your heart is pure before God and man you feel revitalized; wonderful and powerful as your actions reflect universal law.

A pure spirit devoted to ascension is consecrated by the Kingdom of Heaven.

*For those God foreknew he also predestined to be conformed to the image of his Son, that he might be the firstborn among many brothers and sisters.* Romans 8:29

# Soul Tribes ~ Return to Eden

Planets align with ancient prophesies, light code downloads and Twin Flame awakening. This divine symphony is elevating our contribution to resonate in harmony with the song of the Life. We desire only to nurture our souls and live a miraculous life. We made this choice from the urging of the Holy Spirit within.

It is our sacred duty and joy to re establish our sovereignty as children of God. It's time to found human settlements where divine love reigns and Gaia provides a harvest of plenty; in gratitude for our care. Together we create the new golden age.

*You didn't choose me! I chose you! I appointed you to go and produce lovely fruit always.* John 15:16

We are chosen, purified and sanctified by God to live in Christ Consciousness and create the new earth of peace and love as the Father intended. It's up to us brothers and sisters and it's the calling of a lifetime! We are awakening to a truth lost to us for millennia.

A Course in Miracles refers to 'a Cause so ancient that it far exceeds the span of memory which your perception sees.' Is this cause to redeem and save humanity? To be caretakers of earth as we were meant to be? To rise up to a new golden age of love and miracles? My heart says yes.

We are like rose petals opening to Light. The fragrance of divine love unlocks ancient memories of our eternal glory. We are meant to grow in wisdom and bloom in spirit until we have completed our tasks. Then all that is left is the fragrance we shared with the world. Our unique expression of love lives forever in the heart of the universe.

New earth communities thrive near fresh water and grow delicious organic food. We live in gorgeous homes made from and powered by nature. Our homes are private areas where we can just hang out, work on projects or meditate in our privacy of our own gardens. We are all individuals who live our soul calling. Couples live together in love and raise their children in peace. Extended families are also the norm as everyone is cared for. Friends or visitors may share accommodation for companionship.

A welcome and wellness area is prominent, where all can share in spiritual, energy, sound, crystal and herbal healing. Cooking and eating, arts and crafts, music and dancing, praise and worship, learning and teaching, meditating and manifesting areas are central. We all need healing at times so this area is always open.

Founded on Christ Consciousness, there are no leaders as His Holy Spirit is our Guide. The only authority is of parents to raise their children until they are mature enough to walk their own soul path. We are all leaders in the moment. An old man may lead visitors to their accommodations. A child may hum a tune and others sing along. We are designed to coexist in kinship, our individual soul song resonating with all.

*And in Him you too are being built together into a dwelling place for God in His Spirit.* Ephesians 2:22

Some have an aptitude for building, some a gift for creating tasty meals. Others have a talent for swimming and teach that skill to the rest of the group. We are all differently abled. Whatever your natural skills, they are valued and needed.

Children are not forced to learn anything as they are naturally drawn to what they need to know. They show an interest and ask to be taught. They learn through each other, experience, and the wisdom of elders. Humans are born to feel and express a full range of emotions. In the beauty of nature and the loving care of our soul families, they grow in spirit to balanced and healthy maturity as our race heals. Restoration of humanity brings a shared peace of heart not experienced since the dawn of creation. A return to Eden.

The only rule is the golden rule and the only law is universal law. These are known intuitively. There is no money, hierarchy or other false construct. Natural energy exchange is our currency. We connect through the heart chakra; exulting in peace, beauty, abundance and joy.

*Not by might nor by power, but by My Spirit, says the LORD of Hosts.* Zechariah 4:6

Christ Consciousness is all that is needed for full coherence with new earth community. If anyone even thinks about lying, cheating, manipulating or harming others they are immediately directed to the healing area until balance and peace are restored. Some may need to return to the ego matrix to resolve karmic debt. Others never return.

DNA codes are unlocked to remember ancient truth of soul fulfilment. Our collective consciousness is healed as we care for each other and be loving caretakers of Gaia. Universal energy nurtures the earth and her people, creating a sanctuary for all to grow to their full potential.

Here we are known by the name bestowed by our parents from divine inspiration. We may also be known for a certain skill or ability, or for offering a helping hand or a lovely smile. Freedom of expression is natural and exhilarating. Laughing out loud, screaming with ecstasy, weeping with joy, dancing with spirit, rejoicing for all that is holy, and sharing with love.

We are like petals on a flower in the garden of life. As we blossom we recreate our world with miracles of love for the evolution of mankind.

We all hold a part of the mystery of our past and our true potential. Rejoice in the beauty of your brothers and sisters. Rain or shine, we grow together into the eternal souls we are. Loving the eternal in another is true love that lasts forever.

*The fruit of the Spirit is love, joy, peace, patience, kindness, goodness, faithfulness, gentleness, and self-control.*

Galatians 5:22-23

I am blessed with a vision of new earth community. It's the dawn of the golden age and the feeling is exhilaration. Time is again measured by the seasons; the sun, the moon and the stars. All we have to do is be ourselves. Everyone is known by heart and beautiful in our unique expression of divine love.

My vision is at a beach as that is where I feel at home. Ancient ruins by the sea would be awesome to re inhabit, on a private island with fresh water, mountains, caves and a beautiful coastline. A group of women are preparing a feast at a huge covered cooking area, helped by laughing children. The healing area is alive with crystals, art, music, dance, storytelling and human warmth. I'm chatting with Jen who's weaving under shady trees. People are attuned to their own hearts, each other, Gaia and the universe.

Earth is designed to nurture us and is our home during this time in a physical body. We are an inclusive people who can visit or live anywhere. We are welcomed and appreciated, as our unique soul song and experience brings knowledge, awakens ancient memories and restores us to wholeness. Travelling is fun and interesting as each tribe has their unique ways of vibing with the local flora and fauna. By visiting with each other we share our light and learn new skills.

Your heart may be called to snow covered mountaintops or ancient forests. You may travel for a lifetime just because you enjoy it. Live your passion where you are called to be. Soul tribes are planted where they will grow in beauty of spirit. You may spend hours laying in a field watching clouds go by and download a dream to bring to reality, or immerse in meditation for physical maintenance and spiritual growth. Spontaneous action guided by spirit brings dreams to life.

Clothing is optional and made from whatever materials are at hand. You may want to swim naked and sundry your body, before donning a loose robe to join the group. Your tribe may wear grass skirts in tropical areas or woollen pants in cooler climates. This is basic common sense and there is nothing to be ashamed of as we are all family.

> *And they were both naked, the man and his wife, and were not ashamed.* Genesis 2:25

Gaia provides food and medicine for optimal health, materials for housing and is a place of endless wonders where we co create miracles. It's exciting to know we are creating the new earth paradigm, where all who embrace Christ Consciousness live in spiritual bliss and abundance. Aligning our energy with all that is holy transforms us into powerful miracle workers. Soul families sing and dance across the face of our earth to celebrate the freedom of glorious humanity. This is truly the new golden age of higher love!

*You will light each others way - and from this light will the Great Rays extend to shine away the past and make room for His eternal presence.*

ACIM quote from Divine Love Twin Flames by Paula Rule.

The book of Revelation describes the gemstones of new Jerusalem as precious stones that shine in pure light with rainbow colours. Rainbow tribes join in small communities; each one a jewel in Gaia's crown, glowing with love. We are blessed with a world that provides all we need and regenerates itself , we just have to live in harmony with nature and let it nurture us as we care for each other. There is nothing more natural than being your beautiful, angelic self and joining that light with brothers and sisters in spirit.

*Native American Prophecy*

*When the earth is ravaged and the animals are dying, a new tribe of people shall come unto the earth from many colors, classes, creeds and who by their actions and deeds shall make the earth green again. They will be known as the warriors of the rainbow.*

*I AM a child of God - Being what He created me to be – a unique and divine expression of His love. His light lives in me, activated by heart chakra connection with my brothers and sisters. Together our auras glow like a rainbow, realizing the promise and completion of universal love. We are energetically connected to each other, mother earth and the universe to fulfil divine purpose.* Paula Rule

# Journaling

At the beginning of my journey to new earth community; the signs, symbols, dreams and meditation insights had to be recorded to guide me to the Now moment where it all comes together.

This section is for you, dear soul. Your multidimensional identity and mission are ready to be revealed! If you require more space any notebook will do...

Meditation and Dream Journal

*Meditation and Dream Journal*

# Angel Numbers, Signs and Symbols

# My Path to New Earth Community

*My Path to New Earth Community*

*My Path to New Earth Community  ~  93*

## Afterword

Some passages in this book are from Divine Love Twin Flames with quotes from A Course in Miracles; and God, Me and the Mango Tree by Paula Rule.

Sharing for those who want to free themselves from the matrix but are unaware of, or doubt their ability to do so.

I pray all who choose Christ Consciousness complete their soul mission in the joy of new earth community.

Your Sister in Spirit
Paula
goldenraytwinflameearthangel.com

Paula is a Twin Flame, Golden Ray spiritual healer, teacher, writer, speaker, filmmaker, empath, tarot reader and energetic transmuter.

She is an earthangel new earth community founder for Christ Consciousness, Divine Love, Twin Flames, Universal Self, Transcendental Chakras , The 'Clairs' and Rainbow Rays.

*Golden Rays illuminate, creating harmony through universal love. To nurture the seed of divinity in the heart of another is our sacred joy.*

Paula Rule.


goldenraytwinflameearthangel.com

youtube.com/@goldenraytwinflameearthangel

https://onlyfans.com/goldenraytwinflame

Other Books by Paula Rule

# God, Me and the Mango Tree

Paula Rule

God, Me and the Mango Tree

This angel goes through hell on earth to share divine love and awaken to the bliss of ascension. She survived horrific childhood abuse, witnessed the suicide of an eternal love and was saved from death and depravity to share the purest love this world can know.

Her compelling story will inspire you to open your heart for the love of your dreams!

*REAL LIFE, TRUE LOVE AND*
*AUTHENTIC ASCENSION ARE*
*YOUR BIRTHRIGHT!*

# Divine Love ♥ Twin Flames

With quotes from A Course in Miracles

## Paula Rule

## Divine Love ◇ Twin Flames

with quotes from A Course in Miracles·

We are created to remember and embody our sacred universal self through the power of divine love.

So how do we do this? How do we rise above ?

It's all about your soul path ~ the gateway to all truth.

*In each the other saw a perfect shelter where his Self could be reborn in safety and in peace.* A Course in Miracles.

www.ingramcontent.com/pod-product-compliance
Lightning Source LLC
Chambersburg PA
CBHW041501010526
44107CB00049B/1612